WEATHER

Ralph Whitlock

Macdonald Educational

How to use this book

First, look at the contents page opposite. Read the chapter list to see if it includes the subject you want. The list tells you what each page is about. You can then find the page with the information you need.

If you want to know about one particular thing, look it up in the index on page 31. For example, if you want to know about a monsoon, the index tells you that there is something about it on page 13. The index also lists the pictures in the book.

When you read this book, you will find some unusual words. The glossary on page 30 explains what they mean.

Series Editor
Margaret Conroy

Book Editor
Valerie Hunt-Taylor

Production
Susan Mead

Picture Research
Diana Morris

Factual adviser
Dr John Gribbin

Reading consultant
Amy Gibbs
Inner London Education Authority
Centre for Language in Primary
Education

Series Design
Robert Mathias/Anne Isseyegh

Book Design
Anne Isseyegh/Jane Robison

Teacher panel
Catherine Daniel, Steve Harley,
Joanne Waterhouse

Illustrations
Dave Eaton Front cover
Mike Atkinson Pages 16-17, 24, 28-29
Bill le Fever/Linda Rogers Associates
Pages 6-7, 18-19, 22-23
Gary Rees/Linda Rogers Associates
Pages 8-9, 11, 14-15, 25

Photographs
Ace Photo Agency: 12
Camerapix Hutchison Library: 13 top, 28
Daily Telegraph Colour Library: 20
E.T. Archive: 26-27
Susan Griggs Agency: cover
Robert Harding Picture Library: 11, 27
R.K. Pilsbury: 21
Save the Children Fund/Mike Wells: 15
University of Dundee: 25
ZEFA: 10, 13 bottom, 14

CONTENTS

WEATHER AND US

Looking at weather

Have you ever wondered what clouds are made of, why rain falls or what makes snow? This book explains how the weather is made and looks at why it changes during the year.

If you look out of the window, you will see what the weather is like today. The sky may be blue and the Sun shining, or the sky may be covered with clouds and dull. It may even be raining or snowing. How would you describe it?

In some countries of the world the weather stays the same day after day. In others it keeps changing, and it may be sunny one day and raining the next. Can you remember what the weather was like yesterday? Do you wish that you knew what it would be like tomorrow?

People all over the world have reasons for needing to know what the weather will be like in the future. So meteorologists, people who study weather, prepare weather forecasts to tell us.

The weather is very important to all of us. It not only affects what we wear at different times of the year, but also what kind of food we eat, what kind of home we live in and how we spend our time.

When there is a storm at sea, lives can be in danger. This lifeboat is going to rescue people.

In countries where the Sun shines day after day, people enjoy sitting in the shade.

6

This family is eating food flavoured with spices. Spices are grown in hot countries.

What is the weather like today? Do you think it is likely to change? These children think they will need to change their shoes and put on something warm to go outdoors.

What makes weather?

In the morning the Sun rises in the east. In the evening it sets in the west. But it is really the Earth which moves, not the Sun. The Earth turns round on its axis, like a spinning top, and makes a complete turn once every 24 hours.

As the solid Earth turns round, the water in the seas and the air above our heads move with it. Water and air are both called fluids because they flow freely. When a fluid is flowing in one direction it is called a current, and a strong current of air is called a wind. Water, wind and the Sun's heat together make the weather.

The warm Sun heats the water in the sea and turns some of it into water vapour. The vapour rises into the sky, to make a cloud.

Water vapour rising from the sea forms clouds. When the clouds rise higher, over land, they turn to rain. The rain forms rivers and so runs back to the sea. This is called the water cycle.

Sun's heat

clouds

clouds

wind

rain

water vapour rising

sea

river

8

The Earth spins on its axis once in 24 hours, turning from west to east.

The wind blows the cloud across the sky. When the cloud reaches warm land it rises higher in the sky, and meets cold air there. The cold air cools the cloud and turns the vapour into water again. Then the drops of water fall as rain. The rain trickles down the mountains and hills, forming streams and rivers. The rivers flow back to the sea, to begin the cycle again.

You can see the same thing happening in the kitchen. Watch a kettle boiling. Heat makes the water in the kettle turn into steam. The steam escapes through the spout and looks like a little cloud. When it touches the window it condenses, or changes back to drops of water, because the glass is cool.

Steam from the kettle turns to water again when it touches the cold glass.

9

Climate and seasons

Do you remember what the weather was like last Christmas? If you live in a northern country it was probably cold, and it will probably be cold again next Christmas. This is because the weather repeats itself every year as the Earth circles round the Sun. Each journey round the Sun takes a year.

The pattern of weather that a place has every year is called its climate. Each stage in the pattern is a season. The Earth has three main types of climate: polar, tropical and temperate. The polar zones or areas have winter for one half of the year and summer for the other half. Even in summer it is never very warm because the Sun is always low in the sky. The tropical zone has the Sun shining overhead, so it is hot there all the year, with wet and dry seasons.

Christmas in Munich, West Germany, in the northern temperate zone. It has been snowing and the days are short and cold. When it is winter in the north, it is summer in countries, such as Australia, in the South.

Christmas in Perth, Australia, in the southern temperate zone. The sky is blue and the Sun is shining.

In temperate countries the climate is more mild and changeable, and the seasons are of equal length. There are four of them: spring, summer, autumn and winter.

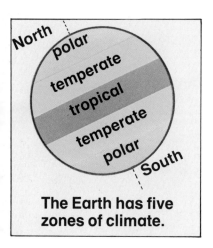

The Earth has five zones of climate.

Many people in temperate countries go on holiday in summer, because the weather is mostly warm. The crops ripen and are gathered in for winter use. In autumn the weather becomes colder and brings rain and gales. The leaves fall off the trees. In America the word for autumn is the 'fall'. Winter is a season for warm coats and gloves because the weather is cold. When spring comes the weather starts to grow warmer again. The flowers begin to bloom and the birds sing and build their nests.

TYPES OF WEATHER

Rain

Rain falls from clouds. The picture on page 8 shows how water vapour from the seas forms clouds. The wind carries the clouds over land, until they turn into rain. When it rains, and how often, depends on where in the world you live. Some countries, which are near the sea, have much more rain than others.

Where no rain falls, no plants can grow and the land is a dry, dusty desert. This is because plants need water to live. All food comes from plants, so it is important to people and animals that plants have plenty of water. We need water, too, to drink and wash in. The water in rivers and wells and from the taps in the kitchen all comes from rain.

Sometimes rain is unwelcome. Here it is interrupting a tennis match.

Sometimes rain is welcome. Monsoon rain helps the rice to grow.

Farmers need lots of rain to make their crops grow. But they do not like rain when their crops are ready to be harvested because too much rain can spoil the crop. Too much rain can also cause floods. This sometimes happens in low-lying land when there has been a lot of rain and rivers overflow.

There are several different sorts of rain. Drizzle is rain made of very small drops of water. It is not much more than mist. A shower is rain which lasts for only a short time. Big raindrops pouring down from a big, dark cloud are known as a downpour.

Thunderstorms, with flashes of lightning, can bring torrents of rain.

13

Sunshine

The Sun is a large ball of fire in space. It is 150 million kilometres away from the Earth, and it gives the Earth enough warmth and light for life to grow. If the Earth were further away from the Sun, its surface would be covered with ice. If it were much nearer, it would be so hot that life would be impossible.

Sunlight helps plants to grow. They need energy from the Sun, together with a gas in the air called carbon dioxide, and water from rain.

If you put a seedling in a pot on a windowsill, it will grow towards the sunlight. If you turn the pot around, the plant will change direction too, and it will soon be growing towards the light again. If you put the pot in a dark corner where sunlight cannot reach it, the plant will grow tall, spindly and very pale. Eventually it will die.

energy from the Sun

carbon dioxide in the air

Plants use sunlight, rain and a gas called carbon dioxide to make green leaves and fruit. Without sunlight no crops would grow.

14

These holiday-makers on a beach in Majorca enjoy the sunshine.

rain

Many people who are going on holiday like the sunshine. They enjoy feeling the warmth of the Sun on their bodies and seeing places in bright sunlight. Some people like to get a sun-tan, though too much sunshine can be bad for you, especially if you are not used to it. It can burn your skin and make you feel very ill.

You should always remember that the Sun is so bright that you must never look directly at it, or you will damage your eyes.

In parts of the world where the Sun shines every day and there is no rain, the land is a desert. Sometimes the rain fails to come in places on the edge of the desert. Then the people living there have trouble finding enough food for them and their animals to eat. Many of them wander from place to place in search of water.

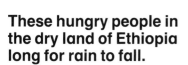

These hungry people in the dry land of Ethiopia long for rain to fall.

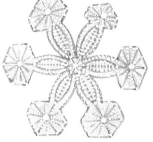

Snow and frost

Is there a pond near where you live? If so, have you ever seen it covered by ice in winter? When the weather is very cold, water freezes and turns to ice. In other words, it becomes solid instead of liquid. Water freezes when the temperature falls below 0° Celsius (or Centigrade). You can measure when this happens with a thermometer.

Snowflakes are ice crystals. Every crystal has a different shape.

Often the air outdoors is mixed with water vapour. At night, when it grows colder, some of this vapour condenses, forming drops of water on grass and leaves and anything cold. We call this dew. In winter, when nights are even colder, the dew freezes and turns to ice, covering the ground like thin snow. This is called hoar frost.

In the upper air it is very cold, but as the snow falls down into the warmer air it often turns to rain.

If you go out in a mist when it is freezing, you may see hoar frost on your friend's eyebrows. Mist is water vapour, just as the clouds are. So you might expect the water vapour of the clouds to freeze, too, when the clouds meet very cold air, and this is what happens. The water vapour freezes and forms very small snow crystals.

Much of the rain that falls started as snow in the cold upper layers of air, but as the crystals passed through warmer air on their way down, they melted and turned to rain. Sometimes, however, the snow does not melt but comes tumbling all the way down to cover the ground. When a heavy snowfall is driven along by strong winds, it is called a blizzard. The snow piles up in huge drifts, blocking roads and covering everything.

Under a blanket of snow and dead leaves, it is warm enough for mice to run about and feed.

Wind

Wind is a current of air. It is air moving in one direction. You can't see air and so you can't see the wind, but you can see what it does to things. Some days there is almost no wind, and the air seems to be calm. But if you wet your finger and hold it up, pointing to the sky, one side will feel colder than the other. That is because the air is moving from that direction.

Have you ever seen a hot air balloon floating overhead? A heater in the basket of the balloon warms the air, and up goes the balloon. Warm air rises and cold air sinks. If you open the refrigerator door the cold air tumbles out, and you'll notice that it is colder near the floor than above the refrigerator. Heat makes air expand, and so warm air is lighter than cold air and rises above it.

In summer the Sun warms the air over the land, making it expand and rise. Sometimes this gives cold air a chance to come rushing in. The temperature falls and strong winds blow, and dark clouds begin to form. Soon rain will be falling, perhaps from a thunderstorm.

In some parts of the world winds blow with such force that they do a lot of damage, uprooting trees, whipping the sea into huge waves and even flattening houses. These winds are called hurricanes, typhoons or cyclones.

When you blow up a balloon, the pressure of the air inside is greater than that of the air outside.

When you untie the balloon, the high pressure air escapes, forcing its way into the area of lower pressure air. This creates wind.

On some days you only have to look at the trees to see which way the wind is blowing. What other things in this picture tell you which way the wind is blowing?

You can lift a plastic beaker by keeping your fingers inside it and pressing against the sides. Air pressure is powerful enough to lift the beaker too. Put a balloon inside it and blow up the balloon. When it fills the beaker, hold the balloon so the air can't escape. Lift the balloon and the beaker will come with it. The air in the balloon is pressing against the sides of the beaker, just as your fingers did, so you can see that air pressure is a powerful force.

WEATHER FORECASTING

What to look for

Will it be fine for the weekend? Would you like to know? All over the world there are people who need to know what the weather will be like, for example, farmers, soldiers and sailors. Can you think of other people who are going to be doing things outdoors and how the weather might affect them?

A hurricane has brought disaster and death to this town in Florida. Forecasting such storms is very important.

People who don't have radio, television or newspapers to tell them about the weather rely on what they can see for themselves. They can tell what the weather will be like in the next few hours by looking at the sky and seeing what sort of clouds are forming.

If the sky is covered with sheets of low, grey cloud, it is probably raining already and the rain may keep on all day. Puffy, white clouds in a bright, blue sky hardly ever bring rain. If they increase until they cover most of the sky, then rain will probably come.

Wispy cirrus clouds may bring rain later.

Wispy clouds, often known as 'mares' tails', are very high in the sky and made of ice crystals. Though the weather is fine, they will probably bring rain in the next day or two. Big billowing clouds, piling up to look like castle turrets, are often signs of a coming thunderstorm.

People who want fine weather for the next day like to see a clear, red sky at sunset. This shows that the rays of the setting Sun are passing through the dust in the air but not through any water vapour.

Puffy cumulus clouds mean fine weather.

Some people are sensitive to changes in the weather, and they become nervous and edgy when a thunderstorm is coming. Many animals and birds are even more sensitive and know when rain is coming, so some people forecast the weather by watching how animals and birds behave.

Low, grey stratus clouds bring rain.

Instruments and measurements

People do not have to make guesses about the weather. They can use instruments to measure the things that help to make it.

The thermometer measures temperature. You should keep your thermometer in the open air but shaded from the Sun.

There are two main scales for measuring temperature. The Celsius (or Centigrade) scale measures temperature from 0°, which is the freezing point of water, to 100°, which is water's boiling point. The Fahrenheit scale puts freezing point at 32° and boiling point at 212°.

anemometer

vane

A weather station has all the instruments for recording and measuring the weather.

NAME				MONTH		
PLACE				YEAR		
DAY	TEMPERATURE	RAINFALL	PRESSURE	WIND	CLOUD	WEATHER
1	4°C	NONE	1030 HIGH	WEST, MODERATE	LIGHT	PLEASANT. BRIGHT.
2	2°C	SHOWERS	980 AVERAGE	NORTH, STRONG	OVERCAST, GREY	SNOW SHOWERS
3	0°C	NONE	1010 AVERAGE	NORTH, MODERATE	NONE	SUNNY, BUT COLD

This chart shows how you can keep a daily record of the weather.

barometer

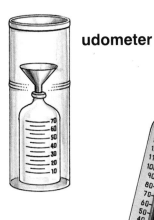

thermometer

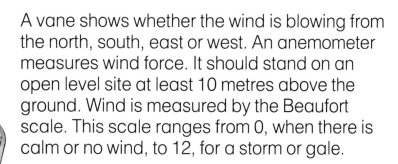

udometer

The barometer measures air pressure. It records the pressure in millibars, 1000 millibars being about average pressure. When the pressure falls rapidly from high to low, rain is likely to fall. A barometer works just as well indoors as outdoors.

A vane shows whether the wind is blowing from the north, south, east or west. An anemometer measures wind force. It should stand on an open level site at least 10 metres above the ground. Wind is measured by the Beaufort scale. This scale ranges from 0, when there is calm or no wind, to 12, for a storm or gale.

The udometer is another name for the rain gauge. An udometer can measure rainfall in either inches or millimetres. It should stand in an open site outdoors so that it does not catch drips from trees.

Daily forecasts

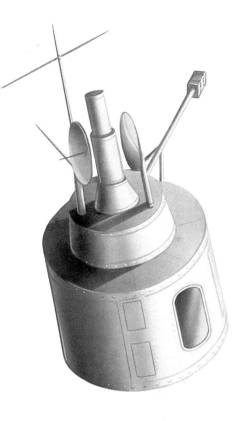

Once everybody had to rely on watching clouds or animals or birds to forecast the weather, but now there are weather forecasts in the newspapers and several times a day on radio and television. We can even telephone for a special forecast for our own area.

Satellites circling the Earth are continually sending back photographs of the clouds beneath them, so meteorologists can study the pattern of the weather taking shape. They can see great swirling spirals of cloud sweeping across the oceans and bringing torrents of rain to the land. Or they can see vast areas of land suffering from drought, with not a single cloud anywhere near to bring a welcome shower.

These same pictures are shown on television so that we can see for ourselves what the weather looks like from Space. Then we can tell whether any large amounts of cloud are coming our way.

A satellite in Space beams back pictures of the Earth's weather.

This satellite photo shows weather when rain is approaching from the north-west.

This map uses symbols to describe the weather shown in the satellite picture on the left.

As well as satellites in Space to send back pictures, there are weather stations in places all over the world. They keep daily records of the weather, noting the temperature, air pressure, wind direction and rainfall, just like you can do on your chart. Some weather stations are on ships at sea, where they are often buffeted by gales and storms. Others are on balloons which take the recording instruments high into the sky. The records are sent back to central weather offices where they are fed into computers. The meteorologists study the records with the pictures from the satellites, and so they can give reasonably accurate forecasts.

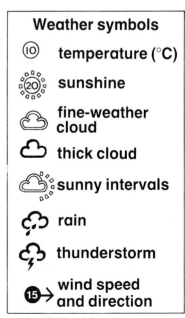

Weather symbols	
⑩	temperature (°C)
⑳	sunshine
☁	fine-weather cloud
☁	thick cloud
☁	sunny intervals
☂	rain
⚡	thunderstorm
⑮→	wind speed and direction

Long-range forecasts

Climates are always changing, though the weather often follows general patterns. For instance, just over a thousand years ago the northern countries of the world enjoyed a warm, mild period for several centuries. The Vikings from Norway and Denmark made bold voyages of exploration across the northern seas during this period of warm weather and even reached America. Then about three hundred years ago England had a series of very severe winters, and the River Thames was often frozen over.

More recently, north-western Europe has had a series of years with fine, sunny weather until late autumn, followed by mild winters and cold, damp weather all through spring. No-one is quite sure of the reason.

Many things can affect our weather. Changes in the Sun itself may explain some unusual weather. The eruption of a volcano may also affect it, because the vast quantity of dust a volcano pours into the air can block out some of the Sun's light and heat.

Forecasters find it difficult to make accurate forecasts for more than about a week ahead. When they want to know if next winter will be cold and snowy, all they can do is to study the records of the past and try to find a year which the present weather pattern matches.

This Frost Fair took place on the frozen river Thames, in England, in the winter of 1813.

As a volcano erupts, it throws great clouds of dust into the air. This can affect the weather, making it colder.

Changing the weather

People all over the world are beginning to worry about the way their activities are changing the weather.

Once, many of the countries in the Middle East and around the Mediterranean Sea were covered with forests. Now most of the forests have been cut down, and much of the land has turned into desert or semi-desert. Vast rainforests in South America, south-east Asia and parts of Africa are now being destroyed in the same way. When the trees have been cut down, animals such as goats and camels eat the fresh shoots that grow from the stumps and so prevent new trees from growing.

Cutting down the rainforest of the Amazon Basin, in South America, is likely to make the climate drier.

In winter it is warmer in cities than in the open countryside. This is because so much fuel is being burnt in a city, including the fuel in cars, that the temperature is raised a few degrees.

Scientists think that we are burning so much fuel all the time, especially coal, that the climate in some parts of the world will become warmer and cloudier, and perhaps wetter. This is because burning fuel releases a lot of carbon dioxide into the air, and it hangs like a blanket over the world, keeping in the heat.

Trees use up carbon dioxide to grow, like the plant shown on page 14. So, many people say that we should not cut down the rainforests, but plant more trees to use up the extra carbon dioxide. What do you think?

In winter, starlings fly to roost in the city at dusk because it is warmer than the countryside.

29

GLOSSARY, BOOKS TO READ

A glossary is a word list. This one explains unusual words that are used in this book.

Air pressure The weight of air pressing down all around us. Where pressure is high, air moves away into places where pressure is low. This makes wind.

Anemometer An instrument for measuring the force of wind.

Barometer An instrument for measuring air pressure.

Blizzard A winter storm, with strong winds and lots of snow.

Carbon dioxide A gas formed from carbon and oxygen. It is produced by us when we breathe, and also when we burn carbon in some form or another, such as coal or wood.

Climate The weather pattern for a place over a long time.

Condense To change from gas or vapour to liquid. Steam and mist condense when they touch something cold like cold glass.

Drought This happens if not enough rain falls in a place for a long time.

Hurricane A very violent storm, in which the winds and clouds swirl around with a circular motion. Other names for it are cyclone and typhoon.

Meteorologists Scientists who study the weather.

Monsoon A heavy rain that always comes at the same time of year in some parts of the world.

Rainforest A tropical forest growing in a region of heavy rainfall.

Rain-gauge An instrument for measuring rainfall.

Satellite A spacecraft launched by rocket, which can circle the Earth and send back weather pictures and reports.

Thermometer An instrument for measuring temperature.

Udometer The scientific name for a rain-gauge; it measures rainfall.

Vane An instrument for measuring wind direction.

Volcano A mountain built up around a hole in the Earth's crust, through which molten rock (lava), steam, cinders, hot dust and other materials are expelled.

BOOKS TO READ

You can find out more about the weather in these books. The first six are easy to read. The last one is a big book written for adults, but with lots of good pictures.

Into the Air (My First Encyclopedia, Volume 9) by Robin Kerrod, Macdonald Educational 1983.

My First Atlas by Michael Weller, Macdonald Educational, 1984.

Weather by Michael Gibson, Hodder & Stoughton, 1980.

The Weather by Frank Dalton, Priory Press, 1977.

The Weather by Bill Bailey, Macdonald Educational, 1974.

Spotter's Guide to the Weather by Francis Wilson, Usborne, 1979.

The Weather Book by Robert Hardy and others, Michael Joseph, 1982.